LACQUER & CRACKLE

**LITTLE
CRAFT BOOK
SERIES**

LACQUER & CRACKLE

by HANNY NUSSBAUMER

**STERLING
PUBLISHING CO., INC.** NEW YORK
SAUNDERS OF TORONTO, Ltd., Don Mills, Canada

Oak Tree Press Co., Ltd. London & Sydney

Little Craft Book Series

Bargello Stitchery
Beads Plus Macramé
Big-Knot Macramé
Candle-Making
Cellophane Creations
Coloring Papers
Corrugated Carton Crafting
Creating Silver Jewelry with Beads
Creating with Beads
Creating with Burlap
Creating with Flexible Foam
Enamel without Heat
Felt Crafting
Flower Pressing
Ideas for Collage
Lacquer and Crackle

Macramé
Making Paper Flowers
Making Shell Flowers
Masks
Metal and Wire Sculpture
Model Boat Building
Nail Sculpture
Needlepoint Simplified
Off-Loom Weaving
Potato Printing
Puppet-Making
Repoussage
Scissorscraft
Scrimshaw
Sewing without a Pattern
Tole Painting

Whittling and Wood Carving

Translated by Manly Banister
Adapted by Louisa Hellegers

The author wishes to express his deepest thanks to Heidi Haupt-Battaglia for revision of the manuscript and for many helpful suggestions.

The publishers wish to express deep appreciation to the Connoisseur Studio, Inc., Louisville, Kentucky, 40207, for assistance and for the photographs from their booklet which appear on pages 10, 11, 12, 14, 15, 30, 31 and 33.

Contents

Before You Begin

Crackle was first considered to be a natural "net-like, cracked pattern in a glaze or in glass." The concept altered slightly to include "*accidental* or *intended* fine cracks in a glaze." It is now possible to produce an authentic-looking crackle finish artificially not only on ceramic glaze, but also on other types of finishes.

Crackle is basically a sign of age and is very becoming on objects styled after their antique equivalents. We are all more or less familiar with this crackle effect, which is often common in old —and even new—ceramic pieces, on old paintings, antique furniture and other items that were at one time or another finished with lacquer or varnish.

These glaze-cracks occur on ceramic pieces when the clay body and the glaze shrink at different rates while cooling, so that the hardened glaze does not fit on the clay. On antique objects, on the other hand, the crackle originates spontaneously and in the course of time through the gradual volatilization—or evaporation—of the oil in the paint. Ultimately, of course, the fine, hairline cracks fill up with dust and dirt and thus become visible at a casual glance. Crackle is, then, actually nothing more than an indication of deterioration. Still, an ancient portrait of, say, an old-fashioned lady, picks up new charm and meaning from a fine, crackle network, which serves only to enrich its appearance. So, profit from these old examples, and decorate anything with hairline crackle!

Opponents of deliberate crackle insist that one should not create artificially what requires generations of natural time to produce. Such an effect, they say, is a false one, and anything that is false is nothing but junk. But, nobody is corrupted simply by wishing to imitate an antique work of art, for a close examination clearly reveals that such things are not old, but have been antiqued by some modern method.

Crackle is, therefore, only a harmless technique for decorating things to get a charming, artistic effect. It helps bring prints of famous art works into harmony with their mountings.

Incidentally, you do not always have to fill the cracks with brown, grey, or another dust-imitating color, but you can also use such colors as orange, green, or even gold, for a striking effect in either setting off a background color, or, simply, in making an impression on the viewer.

Don't spoil your fun by either forming or fighting opinions that are surely stronger than they should be. Just put on an apron and start to work!

Decorating Cardboard Boxes

Apron-clad, you are now ready to choose your base—the object whose surface you want to crackle. For your first project, pick an inexpensive small box—one that you can easily experiment with. You can actually use any type of cardboard, from old scrap pieces decorated and glued onto another object, such as the hangers in Illus. 1, to new boxes bought especially to be crackled.

Applying Ground Color

If you use a new cardboard box, make sure you remove price tags or marks from the cardboard before you begin to work, because it will no longer be possible later on.

Cardboard or pasteboard boxes are usually cream-colored. If you want the ground—or base—to be a different color than cream, paint over it with water-based latex wall paint or, even better, with illustrator's tube colors, poster paint, tempera or gouache, which can be bought at an art supply shop. Add just enough water to whichever paint you choose so the paint is not too thick. Brush the paint on smoothly. Be sure not to make the paint too watery, or you will have to apply several coats. After the color dries, brush

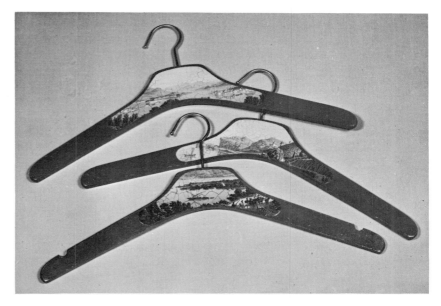

Illus. 1. Decorating old scraps of cardboard is just as much fun as using whole new boxes. The cardboard pieces glued onto these hangers are actually cut-out art prints, applied as on page 16.

7

over it with clear shellac, using a 1″-, 1½″-, or 2″-wide varnish brush to "fix" (prevent the flaking of) the surface. Spray cans of fixatives are available at art supply shops.

To clean brushes used for water-based latex tube paints, poster paints, tempera or gouache, use soap and warm water.

Isolating the Medium

To prepare any medium for crackling, no matter what its shape, you have to isolate or "size" its surface. This means that you brush on a substance, called a sizing or size, which seals the surface.

To size the cardboard box—and, in fact, to size wood or parchment paper—you have a choice of one of three kinds of glue. The first is cellulose wallpaper paste, available in powder form at hardware and wallpaper stores. Stir one heaping tablespoonful of the powder into one pint of water, using a whisk or wire whip, egg beater or electric mixer. Stir briskly until the paste has a uniform consistency. Let the paste stand for 15–20 minutes, then whip it briskly again. It is now ready for use.

NOTE: Mix cellulose wallpaper paste fresh every time you use it, because it thickens very quickly.

The second type of glue is rabbit skin glue, which is available at art supply shops in the form of grains. Put four level tablespoonfuls of the grains into a tin can and add one pint of water. Let the mixture soak for several hours, and then place the container in a hot water bath. Keep the water hot, but not boiling, over a low heat until the glue dissolves. Stir from time to time. The

Illus. 2. Use a soft, flat hog bristle brush to apply glue sizing to the cardboard box.

glue is ready for use when the mixture is completely liquid. Rabbit skin glue made in this way keeps for about a month.

Your third choice of glue is a white glue (such as Elmer's Glue), sold for hobby purposes. This glue is milky white (it is made from casein), but dries clear. It may be thinned with water to a brushable consistency for glueing down paper or for applying to a surface as a size. For this project, it must be thinned with water. White glue keeps indefinitely and requires no special treatment for use.

Apply whichever sizing you decide on to the cardboard with a soft, flat, hog bristle brush, from sizes 2–6, depending on the dimensions of the box.

When the sizing is completely dry, apply a second coat in the same way. This prevents unsightly spots, caused by missed areas, from showing up later on. Be sure to pay close attention to the edges of the box, because if they are not sufficiently sized, later, the lacquer will penetrate under your design and cause ugly blotches.

Clean any brushes you use for glue sizing with warm water.

Attaching a Stick-On Transfer Picture

Now that the box is painted and sized, choose an attractive motif or design to apply. The match box in Illus. 3 has been decorated with a stick-on transfer picture. Lay the motif on the place you want it to be, and carefully mark the positions of the corners with pencilled dots. Using a varnish brush, apply a coat of priming lacquer, sometimes called body or flatting varnish, which is available at paint and hardware suppliers under various trade names. When buying priming lacquer, take

Illus. 3. Lay a stick-on transfer in the still-wet coat of priming lacquer in the position you marked before you lacquered the cardboard box.

care to choose a brand that is thin-flowing and which dries quickly. Let the priming lacquer begin to dry.

Stick-on transfer pictures may be single flowers, bouquets, beetles or, as in this case, birds, and have a protective layer of paper that prevents curling. Dampen one corner slightly and pull the two layers apart from there. Lay the picture, face down, protective paper *up*, on the still slightly wet coating of priming lacquer. Dab it carefully with a wet sponge, until you can push the thin sheet of paper away.

Some stick-on pictures—ships, coaches, and horses for example—frequently have a series of crossed lines on the back to make it easy to stick the picture down correctly. Use the crossed lines for this, but do not be influenced by the picture showing through the protective paper. For this type of stick-on, take the picture by the thumb and forefinger in each upper corner, dip it in water until it is well soaked, and then lay it picture-side *down* on the still wet coating of priming lacquer. Press down carefully with a wet sponge until you can push the paper layer aside. If you see any bubbles marring the picture, stick them with a fine needle to let out the air (see Illus. 4). Press the picture flat with the wet sponge.

Another way to attach a stick-on transfer, instead of laying the picture on the wet coat of priming lacquer, is to brush the picture side with priming lacquer. Wait briefly, until the picture starts to dry and is tacky. Then, stick the picture directly onto the dry box. Press it carefully into place and dab it with a wet sponge to remove the protective paper.

The advantage of this method is that the picture can be applied to projects which require no coat of priming lacquer. The disadvantage is that occasionally traces of lacquer show along the edges of the picture.

The stamp box in Illus. 5 is decorated in still another way. Real postage stamps are set into the wet size coating, before any priming lacquer is applied.

Lacquer . . .

You have already used one coat of priming lacquer to attach the bird stick-on transfer to the

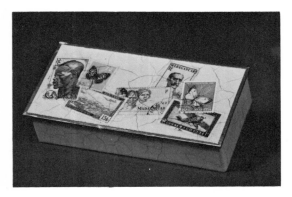

Illus. 5. Real stamps, set into the wet size coating, make an ideal and handy stamp-storage box.

match box. After that has dried completely for at least 12 hours, paint another coat of priming lacquer over the motif and ground color, with a broad, flat varnish brush. It is important to apply both coats of lacquer evenly, because the thickness of the lacquer layer will influence the crackle pattern. A thick coat results in deep, wide cracks and a thin coat in fine, hairline cracks.

Before you finish brushing on the lacquer, hold the box up to the light. Turn it this way and that so the light reflects on every part of the surface. If you see dull spots, they are spots you missed with your brush, so brush over them immediately. If the lacquer is almost dry and is tacky, you cannot brush over it any more or you will ruin the smoothness of the surface.

The second coat of priming lacquer must not dry completely. Let it get tacky, so that, when lightly touched with a finger, it shows a fingerprint. At room temperature, 65°–70°F. (18.3°–21.1°C.), this takes 2–3 hours.

Apply two coats of priming lacquer to the stamp box in this same manner. Clean a brush that has been used for lacquer with acetone or lacquer thinner. If the brush hardens with lacquer still in it, pour some thinner into a tin can and let the brush stand in it for several hours. Wash out the brush in warm, soapy water.

And Crackle!

Numerous brands of crackle medium, often having different constitutions and characteristics, are available. Make sure that both the priming lacquer and the crackle medium you buy are made by the same company and are designed to be used together! Crackle medium keeps about two months, but there is danger of deterioration after that.

Always work at room temperature. With a broad, flat brush, apply the crackle medium over the box in the manner shown in Illus. 6. Then, rub it with the palm of your hand, using light, circling movements, to consolidate the layer. Keep this up until the coat begins to dry, but is still slightly tacky. You must stop as soon as your finger begins to stick. If you do not put the project aside immediately, it will show finger marks.

The crackle begins to form after a short time, perhaps only a half hour. Hold the box up against the light and you should see the action taking place. Remember, though, that you will not see well-defined cracks until you apply color to the crackle.

If, however, within a half hour, you are unable to discover any sign of crackle taking place, or if the crackle appearing is too fine for your purpose, hold the project up to a heater or stove, or put it under an ordinary electric light bulb for a few minutes. This treatment forces the formation of the crackle.

If the crackle still does not appear, the fault is usually with the thickness and the drying time of the previously applied coats of lacquer.

Illus. 6. Brush the crackle medium evenly over the surface with a broad, flat brush.

crackle with circling strokes until it adheres to the crackle (see Illus. 7). Let the box dry for at least 24 hours.

NOTE: Do not add linseed oil to red or green oil paint.

You can use different colors for accentuating the cracks—not only those which resemble dust—depending on the color of the background and the picture. On a dark green ground, for instance, use a light red or orange; on a black or dark brown ground, use a light grey, beige or yellow. Emerald green also produces a very striking effect.

Removing the Crackle Medium

The crackle medium is water-soluble. With a wet sponge, gently wipe the crackle medium off the box, leaving behind only the colored crackle pattern. This procedure is the high point, and your box, at last, sparkles with crackle.

For a final transparent, glossy effect, apply a coat of priming lacquer with a wide, flat brush. Use long strokes and cover the surface completely. Let the box dry, then fill with matches.

Coloring the Crackle

A half hour after the crackle has completely formed, rub color into the fine network in order to make the network pattern stand out more clearly. You can let the project sit for a day or two before filling the cracks without harm to the effect.

Use tube oil colors, mixed with a few drops of linseed oil. Rub the color with a soft rag into the

12

Book Coverings

Art Cards

A unique camouflage for a clumsy telephone book is the crackled book cover in Illus. 8. Artistic greeting cards or other kinds of cards make great book covers, because they mount easily on flat surfaces.

Search through your old Christmas cards, birthday cards and color postcards. Choose one large enough for the telephone book. Cut off any white borders with scissors or, for an especially straight edge, with a paper cutter. Many art cards do not have white borders, but they may have dog-eared or bent corners or small defects along the edges. Trim off any imperfections.

Illus. 8 (right). You will certainly be proud of a handsome cover such as this on your battered old telephone book.

Illus. 9 (left). Transform empty oatmeal or rolled oats boxes into original pencil holders or scrap baskets. Decorate each container with a different art card and then color the crackle appropriately to contrast with the ground color.

Illus. 10. Soak art card in a tray of warm water. If there is no backing, the upper surface of the card is not separated in this way, and you do not need a glue sizing to glue the card in place. Simply use white (Elmer's) glue without thinning.

Painting and Sizing the Book

Paint and fix the telephone book's own cover in the same way you did the cardboard boxes (see page 7). Choose an attractive color which does not overpower, but which complements, the picture.

When the ground and the fixative are completely dry, prepare a sizing as instructed on page 8.

Place the art card in a tray of warm water and leave it there for 1 to 3 hours, depending on its thickness (Illus. 10). Just before you remove the card from this water bath, size the painted book cover (see page 8).

Carefully take the card out of the water. Peel the softened back layer from the art print face (Illus. 11). Simply separate the layers at one corner and pull them apart.

While the picture is still wet, it must be glued to the telephone book, so press it down into the wet sizing coat. If both the card and the book are dry, brush the reverse side of the picture with white glue and then glue it down. With a flat, soft

14

Illus. 11. Remove the art card from the water and carefully peel off the softened back layer.

brush, again size both the picture and the telephone book to keep them from spotting.

Edging and Lettering

Put on the edging round the picture and the lettering beneath it with India ink on the sized surface.

Lacquer and Crackle

When the edge and letters are dry, brush on two coats of priming lacquer and then the crackle medium as you did on page 11. In Illus. 8, the ground and the art card are covered with the same crackle and the same crackle color. Remove the crackle medium (see page 12) and brush on a final coat. You can use priming lacquer for a gloss effect, as you did for Illus. 3, or you can use a semi-gloss lacquer, for a silky lustre, or even a matt-finish lacquer for a matt or dull surface.

After making this telephone book cover, go ahead and create other original projects using art cards.

15

Art Prints

You can obtain art prints either from antique shops, book shops, stationers, or paint suppliers or from art calendars and magazines. Use only those prints that have a blank reverse side. With multi-layered paper called card stock, printing on the reverse side makes no difference, and such pictures are treated as art cards (see page 13). If the reverse side of a print on thin paper has any printing on it, however, do not use it. The printed material would eventually show through.

The address book in Illus. 12 has an artificial leather cover, onto which a piece of cream-colored cardboard is glued, and an art print applied.

Attaching the Print with Sizing

Have your art print ready. The figures in Illus. 12 have actually been cut out from a larger print, but you can attach a whole print in the same way.

Mark the desired position of your print with pencil on the cardboard. Either attach the art print to the address book as if it were an art card (see page 14)—that is, into a wet size coat painted onto the address book, or follow another method. An effective way is to brush the back of the picture itself with sizing, using a soft, flat brush. Let it sit for a few moments. Then, take the two upper corners of the picture between thumb and forefinger of each hand and bring them into line

16

with the two upper, pencilled marks on the piece of cardboard. Carefully stroke the picture downwards until the bottom corners also coincide with their respective pencil marks on the cardboard. Now brush the picture with sizing.

Wipe away any drops of sizing which gather on the edges of the picture with a wet sponge. Let the project dry.

As in the telephone book in Illus. 8, write the dates on this cover with India ink on the sized surface.

Complete the Address Book

Follow the steps for priming lacquer and crackle on pages 10 and 11. Use only a thin layer of lacquer for the fine cracks in Illus. 12. Color the cracks brown as on page 12, apply a final coat—glossy or dull (see page 15)—and let the address book dry completely.

Illus. 13. Be resourceful and salvage an old cigar box. Work a specially selected art print in with the original brand marks and paper seal, then crackle and color the box. The final product shown here is an attractive box to hold paper napkins.

Den Accessories

Wastepaper Baskets

Add an individual touch to useful den accessories with lacquer and crackle. The wastepaper basket in Illus. 14, painted cream, has an art print decoration, which was attached and crackled in the same way as the address book in Illus. 12. After the final coat is dry, add a paper trim round the edge of the basket for an especially unusual look.

Chintz Decoration

The butterflies on the wastepaper basket (Illus. 15 and the back cover) are cut-outs from chintz curtain material. Chintz, a cotton cloth often glazed with wax or some similar chemical substance, is usually imprinted with artistic designs which, when carefully cut out, are particularly suitable for crackle work. Chintz motifs—flowers, butterflies, birds or genre scenes (scenes from every-day life)—often have a printed frame or border. Naturally, you should not cut the frame off, because such borders look especially nice. Chintz is probably easier to handle than art prints on paper.

To apply a chintz cut-out, first paint the cardboard basket to match your décor. Then, fix the surface and size the basket thoroughly with your choice of glue sizing (see page 8). Place the chintz motif in the *wet* size and press the cloth down. Brush over the cloth with the same glue sizing until the weave of the cloth is filled with glue.

Illus. 14. If the delicate facial features in an art print should get a hideous, dark-colored broad crack right through them, twist a tiny bit of cotton round a toothpick, dip it in turpentine and remove the oil paint from the disturbing crack. Take care not to remove color from where you want it to remain nor damage the lacquer undercoat. When you remove the crackle medium, the offending crack will disappear.

When the sizing is dry, proceed with lacquering and crackling (see pages 10 and 11). Illus. 15 has two kinds of cracks—coarse ones on the wastepaper basket itself and fine ones on the chintz picture. Do this by simply applying a heavy layer or lacquer on the main surface, and a thinner one over the art print. If you want, you can accentuate this effect by coloring the two kinds of cracks differently.

Adding a Trim

For a professional and artistic touch, add some brocade, paper or fabric trim, velvet ribbon or a strip of leather round whatever motif you have crackled.

Illus. 15 is trimmed with brocade. Squeeze a track of clear glue from the tube right round the picture, enclosing it in a border or frame. Then, press the trim into place. Be careful *not* to pull the trim tight as you lay it down, or it will arch. Also, do not let it lie too loose or it will buckle. If the trim is wider than $\frac{3}{16}$ inch, also spread the trim's edges with glue.

Start to lay the trim about a half inch below the lower left corner, and continue on, using a single piece of trim all the way around the picture. Do *not* start at the upper right-hand corner of the picture, for that is where the first glance always falls. Where the two ends meet, let one end overlap the other about $\frac{3}{8}$ inch and glue it down after cutting off the excess. If the trim has a wavy or sharp-pointed edge, make sure, in bringing the ends together, that you do not break the rhythm of the design.

Illus. 16. Use ornate art cards to decorate an otherwise ordinary desk blotter.

Desk Blotters

No den is complete without a desk blotter. The crackle part of the blotter in Illus. 16 is made with art cards that have been cut to fit the blotter edges. Follow the same sizing and applying instructions as for the art cards on pages 14 and 15. In Illus. 16, the same large crackle is carried through both the ground color and the pictures, but you can, of course, do otherwise.

The blotter in Illus. 17 was also decorated with an art card motif. As you can see, you can apply parts of the same motif to other desk accessories for a particularly handsome desk set. Draw the black border lines with India ink on the sized surface. Then follow the instructions for art cards on pages 14 and 15. This particular ensemble is not crackled—only lacquered. (See the chapter For Lacquer Only.)

Illus. 17. Here are four projects in one. Cut down several art cards with the same motif to correspond to the size and shape of the individual parts of a desk set.

Parchment—Genuine and Imitation

Genuine parchment is the skin of a sheep, goat or other animal which is specially prepared to be written on. Imitation parchment paper is simply a paper imitation of genuine parchment. You must de-grease both parchment and parchment paper before you can lacquer and crackle them. To do this, moisten a cotton rag with ox gall, which can be bought from an art supply shop.

Size all parchment or parchment paper projects with white glue thinned with water (see page 8), because later, this helps the crackle formation.

Book Covers and Cases

The leather diary in Illus. 18 is smartly decorated with an imitation parchment art card. Attach the card and do the lacquer and crackle in the manner

Illus. 18. Sometimes, you may not be satisfied with the crackle formation—even if it is elegant, fine gold crackle as on this diary cover. Just wash off the coat of crackle medium with a sponge dipped in warm water. After it is dry, brush the project again with priming lacquer—this is the third coat—and re-crackle. If you have already colored the cracks—on the whole project or only on a portion of it—first clean the color away with turpentine, then re-move the crackle medium from the ruined part. Re-coat the entire project with priming lacquer and re-crackle only on the spoiled area.

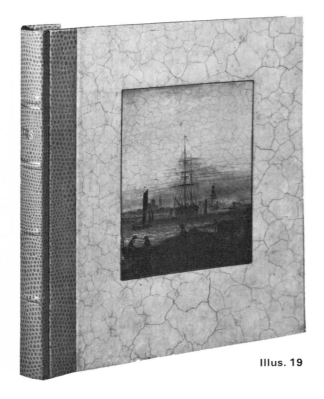

Illus. 19 and 20. Use your imagination to create unique display items such as the imitation parchment photograph album in Illus. 19 and the imitation leather document holder, decorated with a parchment art print, in Illus. 20. Achieve an especially striking effect by using different sized cracks, contrastingly colored, on the background and on the print.

Illus. 19

described on pages 10 and 11. A fine gold crackle color adds the final dignity to this handsome diary.

Art prints also make attractive motifs on parchment. See page 16 for instructions on applying an art print. The photograph album in Illus. 19 has an imitation parchment cover on which an art print is placed. You can experiment with different types of cracks quite effectively on parchment. Lacquer and crackle as usual.

Illus. 20

Lamp Shades

Many lamp shades are made of either genuine or imitation parchment. Combine creativity with thrift—use your imagination to make new shades from any old ones you are ready to throw out.

Art Cards

Each lamp shade in Illus. 21 has been beautifully restored with a cut-out from an art card.

You can use related cut-outs or, for a more modern effect, totally contrasting ones. Size the shades and prepare the art cards as you did for cardboard (see page 14). Lacquer, crackle and then color according to your taste.

Chintz

A chintz motif pressed onto the lamp shade in Illus. 22 adds life to an otherwise plain shade.

Illus. 21. Illuminate a room with this beautiful chandelier; decorate each shade elaborately with an art card and then lacquer and crackle.

If the lamp shade is imitation parchment, lay the motif as you did on the wastepaper basket in Illus. 15. For genuine parchment—and, incidentally, also for wood, sheet metal and glassware—first size the back of the cloth itself, and then lay the picture on a *dry* lamp shade. Wipe any excess sizing away from the edges with a wet sponge. Size the face of the picture evenly so that it will not feel rough when it is dry. Lacquer and crackle as always. The crackle is automatically finer on the chintz than on the parchment paper. Illus. 22 is trimmed with brocade (see page 19).

Patina

Natural patina is a surface mellowing or softening with age. If you decorate a project with a reproduction of an antique painting, you get an especially nice effect if you narrow the contrast between the picture and the surface surrounding it. You can achieve this with an artfully applied patina.

If you do not want to use a picture motif for a particular lamp shade, tint it with a patina. Illus. 23 shows a lamp shade with a light patina applied to genuine parchment.

Use a tube oil color such as brown, which produces an authentic mellow coloring. If the oil paint is somewhat thick, add 3 or 4 drops of linseed oil, so that it flows smoothly. Do not add more than 3 or 4 drops, however, or the color will run too much. Mix well.

With a soft cloth, apply the color to the parchment gently, covering the surface with a circling motion. Use more or less pressure, depending on the intensity of the toning you want. Let the patina dry for 12 hours before you lacquer and crackle it. A single row of brocade trim is all you need to complete the project.

Now that you know the techniques for parchment, use your imagination and skill to make other original items.

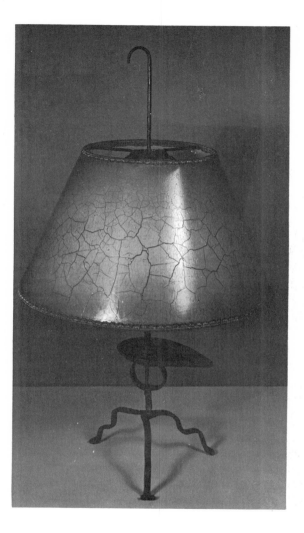

Illus. 23. Add a warm, mellow glow to your living room by applying a light patina to the shade of a table lamp. You may also use patina directly on art prints or other pictures for the special effect you wish. Use bold cracks to complete your masterpiece.

Wood as a Base

Illus. 24. With a soft cloth soaked in turpentine, remove any carelessly placed fingerprints from the edges. Hold the book ends steady with one hand while you rub gently with the other.

Wood is a wonderful, sturdy base on which to lacquer and crackle. Often, in fact, its natural color is attractive enough that a ground color is not necessary. If so, use sandpaper, #0, 2/0, 3/0, 4/0 or 6/0 depending on the wood, instead of paint to prepare the surface.

Book Ends

The book ends in Illus. 24 are natural wood color. If you buy new book ends, use sandpaper to sand off any stamped prices, numbers or trademarks that there may be.

Size the book ends with clear shellac to close

the pores of the wood. Use a soft, flat brush. Apply the shellac evenly, and not too thickly. Clean the brush with denatured alcohol.

NOTE: You can substitute one of the three glue sizings (see page 8) for the clear shellac to seal the wood.

When the shellac is dry, sand the book ends with fine grade sandpaper. If you are going to add any lettering, as in Illus. 24, do so now with India ink.

The figures on the book ends are from art cards. Notice that they are cut out around the figures' outlines. If you do not separate the printed face from the paper underlayer when you glue it down, you get more of a relief effect. Brush the back side of the picture with white (Elmer's) glue and press it down where you want it. Do not apply sizing to the picture.

Brush on two coats of lacquer and crackle as usual. Color the cracks.

Illus. 25. What better storage box could there be for playing cards than a wooden cigar box creatively covered with real playing cards? Leave the trade marks on the box for special effect.

Letter Box

The wooden letter box in Illus. 26 is also natural wood color. The picture on the top is cut from chintz curtain material. Attach the picture as you did the chintz cut-out to genuine parchment (see page 24). Size the rest of the box with clear shellac, and let it dry. Lacquer and crackle. Even though the wood and chintz are evenly lacquered, do not be surprised when they crackle differently. Coarser cracks automatically result on the wood than on the chintz. Color the letter box cracks brown.

Illus. 26. The nature scene in this chintz cut-out is particularly realistic against the natural wood color of the box itself.

Key Chest

A wooden chest, painted and crackled, makes an unusual little closet in which to hang your keys. To paint the key chest, use oil-based woodwork enamel. Apply the paint smoothly and evenly. Fix the surface with clear shellac. When it is dry, sand the wood.

Clean the paintbrush with turpentine (pure gum spirits of turpentine) or sub-turps.

The key chest in Illus. 27 is decorated with an art print. If you choose an art print, place it on the wood with sizing, as on page 27. You can either size the wood first or size the back of the print you are attaching.

This chest is finely crackled only on the picture. You can, naturally, also crackle the chest itself. Color the cracks, add a final coat, and hang your key chest in a handy spot.

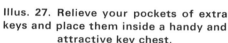

Illus. 27. Relieve your pockets of extra keys and place them inside a handy and attractive key chest.

Sheet Metal Projects

Since sheet metal is a durable substance, you will surely be able to admire your handy work for many years.

Match Box

The match box in Illus. 28 is made of metal. Clean bare or already primed metal—that is, painted or lithographed metal—with turpentine. It is advantageous, when you look for metal to crackle, to choose sheet metal ware that has already been primed or finished. However, if you use bare metal, paint it with synthetic resin (alkyd) enamel.

Clean any brushes you use for enamel with turpentine or sub-turps.

After metal is painted, no sizing is needed. The stick-on transfer picture in Illus. 28 is attached to the first coat of priming lacquer. Apply the second lacquer coat, the crackle and the color as shown on pages 10 to 12.

To remove crackle from the metal box, wash it off with cold water. Add a clear finish, glossy or not (see page 15), with a wide, flat brush. Let the box dry and fill it with matches.

Metal Tray

Decalcomania is the process of permanently fixing a specially-prepared design (decal) to a surface. The metal tray in Illus. 29 is decorated with decals. A decal is different from a stick-on transfer, because it has only a thin covering. A decal is much easier to handle than a stick-on transfer. Decals are especially suitable for surfaces, such as trays, that have been grounded with a dark color. The decals' colors do not lose their intensity when attached to a dark background, as do the colors of stick-on transfers.

First, clean the metal tray with turpentine and then paint it. Let it dry. Then hold the decal, picture side up, by both upper corners, dip it for a few moments in water, and lay it face down on the dry tray. Press it down lightly with a wet sponge. As soon as you observe that the protective paper has loosened from the picture—a little side

Illus. 28. Make a durable and waterproof container for your kitchen matches from a metal box.

29

Illus. 29. Make original decals depicting characters from fairy tales. Crackle when the decal is absolutely dry. If something goes wrong when you crackle your scene, lay the tray in warm water until the coating strips off. Begin again. Crackled projects are washable, but do not leave them in warm water for a length of time.

pressure on the picture will cause it to slip—press with your right thumb lightly on the upper right side of the decal and, with the other hand, carefully remove the paper backing. The decal is sturdier than the stick-on transfer, so do not worry about making mistakes. So long as it stays *wet*, the picture may be moved without trouble into its final position.

In craft and hobby shops, several products for home-made decals are now available. Essentially made of liquid plastic, these products allow you to make your own decals, preferably from color or black-and-white art prints on paper whose reverse side is blank. Such prints are available from art museums or may be taken from calendars. The products can also be used on art cards and picture postcards if the soaking time is extended.

The liquid plastic is brushed on the face of the picture or print in one direction only and allowed to dry. A second coat is then brushed on in a crosswise direction and let dry. Continue in this manner until 4 to 6 alternating coats have been applied. Wash the brush immediately in warm, soapy water, as the dried film is insoluble.

When dry—after at least 6 hours—soak the plastic-coated print in water until the plastic film loosens from the paper. Strip the film and the picture away from the paper. Lay the picture on

Illus. 30 (left). One liquid you can use to create your own decals is "decal-it." Pour out the liquid along the edges of the art print or picture you wish to coat.

Illus. 31 (right). Brush "decal-it" evenly—in one direction only— over the surface.

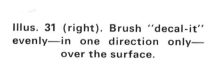

the tray, carefully press it down with a wet sponge, and allow it to dry.

Some home-decal products require that the peeled picture dry first. Then, coat the picture and the tray with the solution and mount the picture. Check carefully which type of product you buy.

Cover the metal tray with two coats of priming lacquer, crackle and color as usual. Remove the crackle as on page 12. Use a clear, heat- and alcohol-resistant finish, such as a polyurethane spar varnish, to ensure a long, well-protected life for your tray.

Illus. 32. Search through stacks of old boxes for interesting shapes to experiment with. A fancy decal, artistically placed, could transform an old pill box into a lovely button box. The fine black cracks and the black trim here are particularly dramatic against the white of the lid.

Glass and Ceramic Ware

You can achieve wonderful effects by treating glass or ceramics with lacquer and crackle. Glass is not porous and does not have to be sized, only scrubbed clean with a detergent and warm water. Rinse well and, preferably, let the glass air dry. A fan can be used to speed up the drying process.

A chintz cut-out, a stick-on transfer or a decal, as in the inside of the glass in Illus. 19, is perfect for application to glass. The bottles on the front cover, originally shampoo and liquor bottles, are artfully disguised by stick-on transfer pictures and decals. If you are going to fill the bottles with liquid, apply a final coat of polyurethane varnish for protection.

Illus. 33. Place a decal inside a glass for a conversation piece you will be proud to display. You may crackle the outside of the glass.

Ceramic is often attractive enough by itself that no design other than a crackle network is necessary. Simply lacquer and crackle the undecorated ceramic as in Illus. 34.

Quite a sophisticated possibility for crackle only is gold or silver crackle. Buy bronze powder, bronzing liquid and poppy seed oil (used for thinning oil colors) from an art supply shop.

Place a half-teaspoonful of bronze powder in a tin lid, add a few drops of linseed oil, and stir with a match stick. Or, add bronzing liquid to the powder, stir, and put in an equal quantity of poppy seed oil.

Illus. 34. Fantastic and intricate crackle patterns develop on undecorated ceramic ware.

You can also buy ready-mixed bronze powder, called "gold paint" or, if silver-colored, "aluminium paint." By the way, numerous other colors of bronze powder are available—red, blue, green and so on. Ask your paint dealer about them.

Clean any brushes you use for bronze powder with bronzing liquid.

Two-Color Crackle

A striking effect on the glass base of the table lamp in Illus. 35 is two-color crackle. Clean and dry the glass (page 33). Then brush on two coats of priming lacquer as usual. Crackle and color the first formed cracks as for any other project. Let it dry for 24 hours. Clean the glass with a wet sponge. Let it dry completely again. Now, apply another coat of priming lacquer. Do not let it dry completely, and apply a second coat of crackle medium. Fill the crackle with a second oil color. Complete the procedure as you do for single-color crackle.

The imitation parchment shade of this table lamp, decorated with chintz cut-outs, is not crackled.

Illus. 35. Be sure to allow sufficient drying time between the various stages of crackle, especially if it is two-color crackle. Never try to hasten drying by putting the project in the sun, by setting it on a heater, or even by placing it in a hot oven, as these cause the lacquer coat to shrink.

Crackle on Hand-Painted Masterpieces

If you have searched through all art supply and fabric shops, and have thoroughly combed your attic, but still cannot find *the* proper decal or *the* right motif, do not despair. Paint your own, right onto the surface you want to crackle! Only one rule: it is urgent that you paint only on sized, completely dry, and—in the case of wood—sanded surfaces! Such surfaces enable you to letter without trouble and without the color running. Use waterproof writing and/or drawing ink (India ink).

Good brushes make the work easy and effective. So, when buying brushes—ox-hair or red sable brushes, No. 0–6 are best—make sure they can be well and easily pointed. To point a brush, dip it in water and form a point between your thumb and fingers.

After a hand-painted creation is dry, brush on priming lacquer, crackle and color as described for each different base material.

Painting on Cardboard

Draw a sketch with a pencil, or trace a drawing with the help of graphite paper. (Graphite paper is intended for transferring designs where erasing might be necessary.) You can make your own graphite paper, using a lightweight layout paper and a stick of soft graphite of degrees 4B or 6B.

Rub the stick over the surface of the paper until the paper is covered with graphite. Then, wipe it down with a paper napkin or rag dampened with lighter fluid (naphtha) or rubber cement thinner. Repeat the procedure several times, until the surface is smooth, velvet black and ready for use as a tracing-transfer paper. Transfer your design, then paint the subject.

Oil paints dry slowly, especially the red colors. Hasten drying by adding half a drop of cobalt linoleate dryer (Japan dryer) per spoonful of paint, or by adding a little burnt umber oil paint to each color. Thinly painted, such colors will be dry by the next day. Colored enamel paints take 2 to 7 hours to dry, depending on the brand, while colored lacquers dry quickly, in up to 2 hours. Acrylic paints dry in 20 minutes when painted on like water color, but thick applications may take even longer—2 or 3 hours. Water colors (including illustrators' colors or gouache and poster colors) dry practically immediately.

To avoid cracking of the painted ground in the following lacquering stage, spray or brush the surface with a fixative or thinned shellac. Use a soft, flat brush. Acrylic colors require no fixative, but may be brushed over with clear, acrylic medium, which, when it dries, is waterproof. Clean brushes used for acrylics with soap and water immediately.

Illus. 36. Painting your own design in colors you choose allows endless possibilities for creative expression.

Painting on Parchment and Imitation Parchment

Sketch directly on the parchment with a pencil or use graphite paper to trace. Paint the design, using water, tempera, poster, or acrylic colors. Oil colors can also be used satisfactorily. Brush or spray the painting with a fixative unless you use acrylics. You can use glossy or matt acrylic medium.

The lamp shade in Illus. 36 is hand-painted. To paint the lamp shade, use colored lacquers, as these are especially strong, light-fast colors. For the best results, let a light shine through the parchment as you paint. When painting a given area, always apply fresh color from the brush to the area most recently painted while it is still wet. If the area is dry, the color will blotch and turn unsightly. Remember, too, that black dries very slowly—check it out beforehand on a trial piece. It may be as long as a week before you dare to lacquer over it without danger of smearing the paint.

Painting on Wood

The wooden jewelry chest in Illus. 37 is hand-painted on the sized and sanded natural wood surface. First, sketch your illustration on the chest with a pencil or trace it with graphite paper. Then, paint. This box is painted with water colors, but you could also use tempera (showcard), or acrylic colors. Always prepare a wooden surface for acrylics by first grounding with acrylic gesso, a priming medium. Let the paint dry.

Wood is an especially gratifying surface on which to paint, because you can erase mistakes! Just let the paint dry, and then sand the mistake away with fine cabinet rubbing paper (a type of sandpaper).

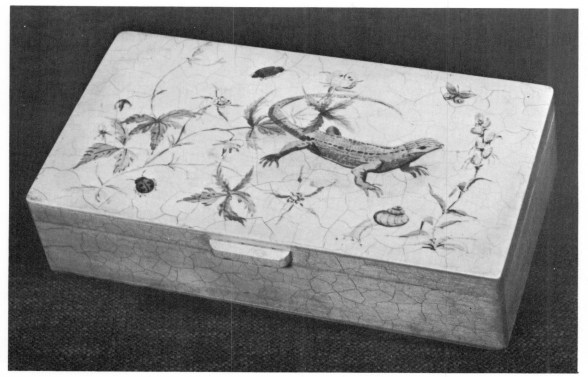

Illus. 37. This natural wood jewelry chest has a light patina (see page 24). To apply a patina, gently follow along the edges of the project with a soft cloth in a circling movement. Proceed from corner to corner, applying more or less pressure according to the intensity of the toning you want.

37

Illus. 38. You will probably hope for crumbs on your table so that you can use this fancy table crumb sweeper to clean them! If you paint with oil, you may shorten the drying time with an infra-red lamp (heat lamp).

Painting on Sheet Metal

If you decide to paint on a metal object, first clean it with turpentine. Then, transfer your outline sketch. If the project to be decorated is light in color, as the tray in Illus. 39, sketch with a 2B graphite pencil or with graphite paper. If the object is painted a dark color, as the table crumb sweeper in Illus. 38, use pastel, Conte or wax crayon.

Paint on the metal. Oil was used in both Illus. 38 and Illus. 39, but colored enamel paints or colored lacquers are also particularly good for this.

Wipe away small mistakes with a brush dipped in turpentine. Larger mistake areas can be cleaned with a turpentine-soaked rag.

You can wipe off a water-based painting in a similar way, but use water instead of turpentine. An acrylic painting, though made from a water-based paint, is waterproof when dry, and, hence, cannot be washed away. If you wish to replace the painting with another, paint over the first one with two or three coats of acrylic gesso (enough to hide the underpainting). Let the gesso dry, then go ahead and do your second painting on top of the first.

Illus. 39. Be daring when you paint on metal because, if you wish, you can easily erase your design and begin again.

Painting on Glass

The large bottle on the front cover is delicately hand-painted with cherries. To paint on glass, first clean it with hot water and a detergent. Transfer your sketch with wax crayon, or glue the sketch to the back side of the glass you intend to paint. Notice that the thicker the glass, the harder it is to follow the outlines of the sketch. Always look straight through the glass at the line being traced, never at an angle. If viewed from one side, the real position of the line will be distorted by the bending of the light rays as they take an angling path through the glass.

Paint small motifs—single flowers, little hearts, playing card designs—directly on the glass. Colored enamel paints or colored lacquers (which are used for the cherries) are most suitable for this. You can buy these paints very inexpensively in jars as tiny as $\frac{1}{4}$ fluid ounce. Stir the paint well before and during use. A match stick is quite good for this. If the color thickens slightly, thin it by adding a few drops of mineral spirits for enamel or lacquer thinner for lacquer.

You can also paint on glass with tube oil colors. Oils are particularly suitable for flowers done in an antique style.

For Lacquer Only

As complex as the whole process of crackling is, the process of only lacquering is just the opposite. Lacquering takes only three words to describe: Omit the crackle! If you reject the idea of crackle on whatever grounds, you can ignore that part of the work completely and content yourself with plain lacquering.

If you reserve crackle mainly for those projects decorated with antique motifs, you can use simple lacquering especially on articles of modern design. For example, Illus. 40, originally a plain cardboard box, perhaps from dry cereal, is now an attractive wastepaper basket. This type of box may have an uneven or rough surface which can easily be painted, but which does not crackle well. Here, cut-out chintz animals are placed in a wet size coat (see page 18). When dry, lacquer only.

Illus. 40. Chintz animal cut-outs make a fun wastepaper basket for a child's nursery.

Illus. 41. Even a child can paint a simple, original design on a tin can. The converted cigar box on the right still has the original trade mark decoration as a border for the art card.

String Box

Transform a small tin or aluminium can that has a tight-fitting, inset lid into a useful box to hold a ball of string. Clean and paint the metal (see page 29). After you decorate the can, punch a hole in the bottom with an ice pick and hammer the projections flat. Bring the string out through the punched hole. Lacquer only.

Illus. 42. Re-use cylindrical cardboard cereal containers either in full length, as wastepaper baskets, or, as shown here, in half length, as sewing baskets. Decorate the basket with a stick-on transfer, lacquer it, and line it with chintz.

Illus. 43. The hand-painted wooden plate (done with water colors on the sized surface) is not crackled and the natural grain of the wood shines through beautifully and clearly.

Illus. 44. Bring a bit of nature permanently inside your home. Press plants and carefully set them into a coat of wet priming lacquer.

Pressed Plants

Try a completely different motif that need be —in fact, must be—lacquered only because it cannot be crackled—pressed plants.

Gathering the Plants

Meadows, woods, pastures, and even your own yard offer an inexhaustible supply of "press-worthy" plants—all potential crackle motifs. The assortment of blossoms, flowers and leaves is so great that you should not have to use those rare species valued by conservationists in order to get suitable items. Even a dried weed can be a beautiful, natural design.

Take a notebook and go for a walk. As you pick your specimens, carefully lay them between the pages, shutting the book gently so you do not tear the flowers.

Pressing Your Specimens

At home, spread your collection on blotting paper or, if the leaves and blossoms do not contain much moisture, on plain (unprinted) news-print paper, available from art supply shops. Slightly withered plants are the easiest to spread out. Therefore, wait a while—never press freshly picked plants. Arrange the plants according to their thickness and weight them down between blotters or papers with as many books as are needed. Keep a good watch on how well the pressing is going. Occasionally, change the blotters or papers, relieve some of the weight where it seems too much, and add to others that seem not to have enough. Judge all this for your-

self from the condition of each individual plant. You can achieve the widest range of color gradations with delicate pressure.

Attaching the Plants

Prepare the project as you would to decorate it with any other motif—paint it, if you wish; size it, if it is not metal or glass; and sand it, if it is wood. Then, brush the project, no matter what its composition, with priming lacquer, even if it has already been given a coat of size. Using tweezers, lay the well-dried plants into the still-

wet coat of lacquer. Let it dry. If a flower stem breaks loose from its position, stick it back on with clear glue when the lacquer is dry. Also, if any of your flowers have suffered a strong loss of color, either because of their original delicacy or because they have been stored too long, you can freshen them up by applying a light tint of water color. Only tint, *do not* color. Otherwise, the effect you get will be an unnatural one.

Size the lacquered plants with cellulose wallpaper paste, using a soft, flat brush. You may substitute rabbit skin glue sizing, or white (Elmer's) glue, thinned with water, as a sizing. Remember that the white glue dries clear. This sizing is not absolutely necessary, but it does preserve the natural look of the plants. Let the sizing dry.

Now, brush clear lacquer over the entire surface, including project and plants. Use a semi-gloss lacquer and apply two or three coats, allowing each to dry before proceeding with the next.

Finishing the Project

When you do not crackle, you may, however, add other finishing touches. For example, rub on a patina. Add a trim. Or, carefully crackle around the plants, as in Illus. 46.

Now, you know the basic rules. Use your imagination to mix-and-match the many possible base surfaces and the comparable number of decorative motifs. Whenever a piece of "worthless" material shows up, put it aside to lacquer and crackle. If you take the trouble to beautify this "worthless" material, whoever receives such a gift is bound to think you had to reach a bit deeper into your pocket than you actually did!

Illus. 46. Save yourself the job of folding table napkins by stacking them in this unusual table napkin holder for guests to help themselves. A crackle network surrounds the pressed plants.

Illus. 47. Here is another project, especially if you are ecologically minded. Instead of discarding an empty stationery box, decorate it with pressed plants and use it to keep gloves or knickknacks in.

Index